The Natural Speaker

The Art of Going From Fear to Fearless, And Leaving Them Speechless in the Process! Simple Steps That Will Change Your Life!

Yael Eylat-Tanaka

The Natural Speaker

*The Art of Going From Fear to Fearless,
And Leaving Them Speechless in the
Process!*

Simple Steps That Will Change Your Life!

Yaël Eylat-Tanaka
(Distinguished Toastmaster)

Copyright

ISBN-13: 978-1530133840

ISBN-10: 153013384X

Published by Yael Eylat-Tanaka, Tampa, FL

Email: Prowriter33@gmail.com

Website: http://Pro-Wordsmith.net

Please feel free to contact me, to give me your impressions of the content, to write a review on Amazon, or for anything else.

Other Books by this author

Common Bits of Life
Lake of Silence
The Book of Values
The Compact Book of Values
Diet Proof Your Life
Diet Proof Your Life Action Book
Publish Your Book Using CreateSpace
Publish Your Book on Kindle
Publish Your Book on NOOKpress
Publish Your Book on BookTango
Publish Your Book With Smashwords
Publish Your eBook Your Way!
SCREAMS!
Revenge of the Cat Woman
It Ain't The Money!
Time Travel
The Natural Speaker
The Burning Heart (Out in March 2016)

Contents

Introduction

There are countless books and websites dedicated to the art of public speaking. Many of them are excellent. So why another one? Indeed, why talk about public speaking at all?

Public speaking is arguably one the most dreaded activities we ever engage in. It is described by psychologists as being second only to death in the degree of anxiety it produces. Paradoxically, it is also an activity we all engage in all the time, every day, and in many different ways.

I wish to dispel the grip of fear that so many experience when considering public speaking.

About thirty years ago, I became aware of my own fear – not of public speaking, but of public singing. I could not overcome my anxiety at having my voice break, or holding a note long enough to have my lips twitch, or belting out my voice with such power where my tonsils showed up on a close-up. Such considerations haunted me. I would sit curled up on my sofa dreading so much as the possibility of being so vulnerable.

That was not a comfortable experience. I did not enjoy such self-consciousness. It did not feel right. It did not feel good.

I realized, too, that I did not have to sing in public. Funny how some self-imposed imperatives are about as unrealistic as growing wings! Once I recognized that my anxiety was self-imposed, I dipped my toe into a semi-public milieu, and signed up for private voice classes. I would thus have to stretch a bit, and sing in front of one other person – my teacher.

To say it was easy would be a gross misrepresentation. On our first meeting, she asked me to sing a familiar song, "...just to see where you are." Hmm. I croaked out some timid notes, having vowed that I would overcome this fear. I persisted with my lessons. Then, an epiphany: I would join Toastmasters.

I appeared at a meeting, was introduced to the group, signed up as a member, then spent an entire year blending into the background before getting up to give my icebreaker speech. A full year.

Toastmasters is an international organization dedicated to helping people improve their public speaking skills through a series of exercises from manuals, thus advance through the ranks as they accomplish various necessary steps in their growth. The first manual of ten speeches, beginning with the introductory icebreaker, took me about two years to complete. I gave each of the first nine speeches after having written it, practiced it, memorized it, then standing at the lectern clutching it for dear life, reciting my speech through cantankerous butterflies and Jello knees.

It was misery.

Then I reached the last speech.

To this day, I remember the project topic. It was on critiquing, or what we now call evaluations. I read through the manual instructions, took notes, and tried to fit a proper speech into the given outline. It was the proverbial square-peg-into-a-round-hole attempt. There was something wrong: With my degree in psychology, I fundamentally disagreed with the premise presented in the manual. How shall I prepare my speech so it fits the manual's instructions? I struggled with that, wrote and rewrote my speech, and then took a big leap into foreign territory.

The evening of the speech I joined some members of the club at the bar before the start of the meeting. We drank a few beers and then ambled into the room for the usual preliminaries.

Then came my turn at the lectern. I grasped it with white knuckles, looked at the audience, and gave my opening line: "I disagree with the manual."

What?!

Nothing happened. I was not strung up by my thumbs for veering off the path. I was not condemned for daring to voice my opinion. In fact, I had the group's rapt attention as I proceeded to support my statement. I enlisted one of the members to help me demonstrate my point, and together we were so effective that we got a standing ovation.

And I found my voice.

4

The Many Faces of Public Speaking

You may well ask, *Why should I learn public speaking? I have no intention of ever giving speeches!* In fact, the skills learned with public speaking encompass much more than merely giving speeches. Consider, for example, the following areas in which poise and effective communication can go a very long way in establishing you as an expert in your field:

- Disseminate complex information with ease.
- Mediate conflicts.
- Learn to give online webinars.
- Conduct effective meetings.
- Get to the point easily.
- Be effective in rallying your team.
- Be able to influence people.
- Be effective at a job interview.
- Learn powerful sales techniques.
- Negotiating skills.
- Speak on radio or television.
- Participate in a play.
- Speak to management.
- Improve interpersonal communication.
- Give a toast or speak in praise.

These are just examples of the areas that can be improved with communication skills. Each of the above areas – and more – demand a level of confidence when speaking. Whether you are on stage delivering a formal speech, or speaking one on one with a prospect, communication is key.

What is Communication?

As human beings, we enjoy a unique talent not shared by the other animals: We can think and speak. However, although many of us assume that communication means speaking, it actually encompasses far more than merely making sounds with our mouths. Just as the animals are able to communicate a great deal with their bodies, their eyes and their behavior, so, too, human communication is based on many levels, including the less obvious "body language." Consider the message given by simply rolling one's eyes, or a limp handshake, or turning one's back on a prospect. No words need be spoken, yet the communication is undeniable.

Public speaking incorporates all the communication skills one has, from eye contact to one's personal space. Have you ever experienced a sales person who stands too close or speaks too loudly? Were you able to concentrate on his or her message, or did you wish to escape? Have you ever experienced a professor who spoke too softly? If hearing the lecture was a challenge, where was your attention – on the subject matter or on straining to hear?

When we watch politicians campaign, it is not merely their words that appeal or repel us: It is their body language, their facial expressions, their authenticity in presenting themselves. Nothing turns us off more than lack of genuine presence. A forced smile is immediately apparent; an insincere response is quickly discerned and off-putting; cruelty and mockery are often rejected. We associate vicariously with the speakers; we empathize and root for them when they are genuine; we reject them when they try too hard.

Public Speaking – The Second Most-Feared Activity

Psychologists have determined that of all fear-inducing activities or objects, public speaking rates right up there with death. Not snakes or drowning; not dread diseases or loss of economic security – public speaking.

That is not to say that people are not concerned about serious illness or loss of money. What it says is that as a whole, people experience much greater angst when faced with the prospect of public speaking than any other endeavor or agent, save, perhaps death.

That is curious, in the face of the dire consequences that issue from some of these: With the loss of money, one's economic security is in jeopardy. With a serious illness, one's lifestyle, economic security, family and very existence can be in jeopardy. The loss of a spouse, a job – you get the gist.

But public speaking?

Consider what fear is: It is the reptilian brain's instinct to protect oneself. As primitives, humans existed in small groups, hunting together and staying together in small caves. There was a great deal of danger all around. Our very survival depended on being vigilant. That is the nature of fear: to protect us from mortal danger. But even as we evolved into our modern life, our primitive brain did not evolve at the same rate, and our base emotions are still raging, from fear to anger and other instinctive reactions.

Public speaking is not a source of mortal danger. There are no tigers nipping at our heels, no snakes crawling underfoot. And yet we react as if there were.

What are the consequences that can issue from public speaking? The most dire or potentially embarrassing consequences might occur if one stuttered or forgot one's stream of thought or was so petrified as to freeze in one spot or run off the stage.

Is that a fear worth its status of ranking just below death? To be sure, personal embarrassment may well figure quite highly on a fear scale, but that, too, could and should be challenged.

The Origins of Embarrassment

Remember the story of my own fear of public speaking? I told the story of being paralyzed by fear of singing in public. That was my original impetus for joining Toastmasters. I was so determined to overcome my fear that I wrote essays and blog posts about it. I watched *American Idol* to learn what set apart the winners from the wanna-be's, and cringed when some with a horrible excuse for a voice dared to audition. In public, no less! Before professional judges! Some of the performances left me aghast!

There was something they all had in common that I did *not* wish to emulate: They all belted out songs with contorted facial expressions presumably designed to eke out emotion and project their voice as they held out notes. I wanted none of that. Even opera singers displayed similar characteristics: contorted facial expressions, trembling lips, teeth and uvulas prominently displayed on the screen by close-up camera shots!

Ugh!

No, that was definitely not what I was looking for.

We all want to appear wonderful, in control, poised, "with it." Unfortunately, we also are all human.

There is no question that some of us are confident, rich and perhaps cocky, but dig a bit deeper, and we all suffer some universal imperfections. If one is a terrific student, he or she may be shy; if one has a lot of money, he or she may have been abused as a child or adult; if one is blessed with a very handsome or beautiful spouse, he or she may be plagued with a dread disease; and so on. The frailties of humanity do not need to be dramatic, but they are universal. Just because someone *appears* to have it all together does not mean he or she actually does. Bear in mind that everyone has strengths and weaknesses of some kind. No one is immune – not the president of the United States, not the Hollywood star with the most Oscars, not even the Queen of England. Yep, even the Queen has her insecurities.

Once this lesson is firmly planted in your mind, you will feel an enormous release from the grip of perfectionism.

It is perfectionism that makes us stumble and fall. Our desire to appear perfect to the world is an attempt to hide our insecurities. Do you feel self-conscious about your looks? Are you afraid that someone will discover some of your secrets? Do you have skeletons in the closet that you fear will be revealed?

We all do! Everyone, from every corner of society has those fears. You are not unique.

Once you understand that concept, nothing you do or say will ever again have power over you.

I competed (successfully) in the Humorous Speech Contest that is part of the Toastmasters repertoire. But deciding to compete in the first place was not without pain. I remember talking to a friend, and sharing with her a memory I had from thirty-five years earlier. I shared also that I wished I had the nerve to give that speech because it sure was funny at the time, but I did not dare. When I told her the story, she laughed so hard, she could hardly catch her breath. She then said, "People pay money for that!" implying that the material was so genuine – and funny – that I had to compete. It took all my courage, but in the end, I gave the speech and won first place at one level and second place at a higher level.

But do you know what is even better than winning at any level? I overcame an enormous self-imposed obstacle about sharing a perfectly natural and very funny episode.

What is Public Speaking?

Everyone speaks, all the time, with a lot of different people, in many situations – on the job, on the phone, to one's family and friends. You speak to your parents, you speak to your boss and colleagues, you participate in class, or you enjoy a dinner out with some buddies. Every single one of these situations requires you to speak in public! But none of those situations puts the fear of God in you because they are so familiar. You speak spontaneously, with a give and take, with others interrupting and interjecting their own ideas into the conversation; you may leave some things up in the air; or you may find yourself forcefully pushing your point of view on the group. All of these situations involve spontaneous speaking.

What brings people to their knees is the concept of preparing a formal speech to an audience. In fact, you always have an audience of some kind; but you do not always have to *prepare* your speech. Even in the event of applying for a job where you may have an important interview, you can rarely anticipate the kinds of questions you will be asked, and thus prepare a 30-second blurb.

If you speak about what you are familiar with, you will have countless topics to talk about; if, however, you select a topic about which you know nothing, you still struggle when writing it, when practicing it, and when delivering it! For example, I could no more talk about extreme sports than I could fly to the moon. But I can say volumes about nutrition or my life growing up in the Mediterranean.

The Most Important Lesson

Far and above any other technical instruction you may receive is that you must speak about what you know.

I am not suggesting that you obtain an advanced degree on your topic; I am suggesting that we each have a stable of topics about which we know something, or feel strongly about, or have opinions about. If you are a passionate sports fan, speak about your favorite sport; if you are sizzling with opinions about politics, by all means, expound on that; if you, like me, love classical music, tell your story from that vantage point.

Whatever your interests, that should be your focus. Are you a crackerjack baker? Explain the finer points of bread making or frying doughnuts. Love horses? Tell your audience what is so wonderful about those powerful animals.

Which brings us to the next matter:

Is Toastmasters The Answer?

I have mentioned Toastmasters International several times throughout this book; however, I want to make it clear that Toastmasters is not the only game in town. To be sure, it provides invaluable benefit to its members, with instructional manuals, videos, over fifteen thousand clubs worldwide, offering its members support, leadership and camaraderie.

There are several other organizations that teach public speaking, including colleges and universities, your local theater, Dale Carnegie, Inc., National Speakers Association with chapters in every state and many cities, as well as private companies. Each enterprise has a slightly different focus, with the main intent being on improving presentation skills and increasing confidence. As in all things in life, you should be clear on your own needs, and then search out those concerns that best emphasize and bolster those needs. In fact, why not check out several?

In addition to speakers organizations, there is also a plethora of information that can be gleaned online. One of my favorites is www.ellenfinkelstein.com. Ellen Finkelstein is an author, speaker, and trainer, and I especially like her description of the charismatic speaker. Take a look at the following list of qualities that she describes:

- Charismatic speakers are **self-confident and assured**. They don't appear nervous or ill at ease.

- Charismatic speakers seem to be enjoying themselves; they are playful, humorous, **happy**.

- Charismatic speakers are **lively** & energetic.

- Charismatic speakers are **knowledgeable** about their subject.

- Charismatic speakers **look good**, they have a stage presence.

- Charismatic speakers **speak without stumbling**, using full sentences and correct grammar, without "ers" and "uhs."

- Charismatic speakers have an **opinion** about their subject. They care about it. You can sense their emotion, enthusiasm, and conviction.

- Charismatic speakers relate their topic to the broader scheme of things, they are expansive, **inspiring**, and uplifting.

- Charismatic speakers create a strong **rapport** with their audience, they connect.

- Charismatic speakers are **positive** in outlook, cheerful, and cooperative.

- Charismatic speakers are **organized**; their points are clearly connected and logically follow one another, with an overview at the beginning and a conclusion at the end. They are precise and complete.

- Charismatic speakers (genuine ones) are **honest**, well mannered, patient, fair, and responsible."

(http://www.ellenfinkelstein.com/pptblog/12-steps-to-becoming-a-charismatic-speaker)

Toastmasters International has put together a set of manuals designed to take a budding public speaker through various stages of speech-giving, from the very elementary to the more advanced. The very first speech a newbie is asked to present is the so-called Ice Breaker. This is presumably the easiest speech of all, because the newly-minted Toastmaster can give a very short autobiography. He speaks about himself! What could be easier than that? Talk about a subject he knows plenty about!

But …

When we say the words "public speaking," many people automatically think of standing before a large crowd of critical people with their arms crossed in front of them, looking at you and waiting for you to stumble as you deliver an hour-long dissertation. But that rarely happens.

The Manual Path

If you are reading this book, then you are probably new to the game. Yes, it is a game. In the world of Toastmasters, the initial manual with which newcomers are presented is made up of ten speech projects. Each project emphasizes a different aspect of speech giving. For example, earlier I mentioned that the very first speech is the Ice Breaker. This is where the newcomer is given four to six minutes to speak about him- or herself. It is a mini autobiography. It is a self-introduction.

The Ice Breaker should be one of the easiest speeches to give, yet has given many people the shivers. What shall I talk about, they ask? What can I say about myself? It took me a full year to get up the nerve to stand before the group and introduce myself! I clutched the lectern with white knuckles throughout the subsequent eight speeches until I discovered the magic bullet. It is my wish to lessen the pain for the reader.

Applying Your Skills

The following are the current list of ten speech projects in the Toastmasters Competent Communicator Manual:

1. **The Ice Breaker** – the speaker introduces him- or herself to the group.
2. **Organize Your Speech** – this project encourages the speaker to present his or her topic in an organized fashion that the audience can easily follow.
3. **Get To The Point** – similar to the previous project, this project teaches the speaker to be concise, rather than rambling.
4. **How To Say It** – asks the speaker to utilize the best words or phrases to present his or her topic to best effect.
5. **Your Body Speaks** – movement around the speaking area, gestures, eye contact.
6. **Vocal Variety** – addresses volume, pitch, rate of speaking.
7. **Research Your Topic** – here, the speaker is asked to present a speech where some rudimentary research has been conducted, say, on how to bake a cake or equipment needed to go camping.
8. **Get Comfortable With Visual Aids** – the speaker may use a board or slides or any prop that will support his or her topic.

9. **Persuade With Power** – the speaker is asked to present a topic about which he or she is passionate enough to affect public opinion.
10. **Inspire Your Audience** – the speaker is asked to appeal to the noble sensibilities of the audience.

As you read through these ten projects, you will note that no topic is given for the projects. That is up to the speaker. These projects simply reflect a roadmap of specific skills to be learned and practiced.

According to Toastmasters, each subsequent speech project is meant to build on the skills of the previous speech, and reveal areas that need work. The dedicated speaker will repeat a speech until he or she feels they have mastered its objectives.

An important point to keep in mind is that these manual speeches are five to seven-minute speeches. That's it. Not until a speaker gets to the advanced manuals do the speeches require longer presentations.

The Advanced Manuals

Once you complete the Competent Communicator manual of ten projects, you are presented with a certificate of accomplishment and the designation Competent Communicator. Believe me, it is a proud moment to reach that achievement. You have learned some skills, polished some others, and completed a course of study. The most impressive and influential accomplishment of all, however, is that you have overcome your fear of standing before a group and speaking.

I cannot impress upon you the rush of joy that provides!

And if, like me, you found your "self" in the process — what kinds of speeches you like to give, what is your style of preparation, your style of addressing the audience and other subtle applications, nothing can compare to the feeling of joy that you experience.

Once bestowed the Competent Communicator designation, a member may move on to the advanced manuals. Advanced projects emphasize various aspects of public speaking which hone areas of specific interest to the speaker, such as theater acting or performing on radio, presenting a technical topic to company CEOs, or polishing one's ability with humor. The following is a list of the current advanced manuals offered by Toastmasters International:

The Entertaining Speaker

1. Sources for Entertainment 8–10 min
2. Make Them Laugh 8–10 min
3. A Dramatic Talk 10–12 min
4. Speaking After Dinner 13–15 min

Speaking to Inform

1. he Speech To Inform 5–7 min
2. Resources for Informing 8–10 min
3. The Demonstration Talk 10–12 min
4. A Fact-Finding Report 10–12 min
5. The Abstract Concept 10–12 min

Public Relations

1. The Public Relations Speech 5–7 min
2. Resources for Goodwill 8–10 min
3. The Persuasive Approach 8–10 min
4. Speaking Under Fire 6–8 min
5. The Abstract Concept 8–30 sec

Facilitating Discussion

1. The Panel Moderator 28–30 minutes, alternatively 22–26 minutes
2. The Brainstorming Session 31–33 minutes, alternatively 20–22 minutes
3. The Problem-Solving Discussion 26–31 minutes, alternatively 19–23 minutes
4. Handling Challenging Situations 22–32 minutes, alternatively 12–21 minutes
5. Reaching a Consensus 31–37 minutes,
6. alternatively 20–26 minutes

Specialty Speeches

1. Speak Off the Cuff 5–7 min
2. Uplift The Spirit 8–10 min
3. Sell A Product 10–12 min
4. Read Out Loud 12–15 min

5. Introduce The Speaker Entire Meeting

Speeches by Management

1. The Briefing 8–10 min

2. The Technical Speech 8–10 min

3. Manage And Motivate 10–12 min

4. The Status Report 12–15 min

5. The Adversary Relationship 5–15 min

The Professional Speaker

1. The Keynote Address 15–20 min

2. Speaking To Entertain 15–20 min

3. The Sales Training Speech 15–20 min

4. The Professional Seminar 20–40 min

5. The Motivational Speech 15–20 min

Technical Presentations

1. The Technical Briefing 8–10 min

2. The Proposal 8–10 min, 3–5 minute Q&A

3. The Non-technical Audience 10–12 min

4. Presenting A Technical Paper 10–12 min

5. Enhancing a Technical Talk with the Internet 12-15 min

Persuasive Speaking

1. Conquering the Cold Call 10–14 min

2. The Winning Proposal 5–7 min

3. Addressing The Opposition 11-12 min

4. The Effective Salesperson 8–12 min

5. The Persuasive Leader 6–8 min

Communicating on Television

1. Straight Talk 3 +- 30 sec

2. The Talk Show 10 +- 30 sec

3. When You're The Host 10 +- 30 sec

4. The Press Conference 4–6 min, 8–10 minutes Q&A

5. Training On Television 5–7 min, plus 5–7 minutes for playback

Storytelling

1. The Folk Tale 7–9 min

2. Let's Get Personal 6–8 min

3. The Moral Of The Story 4–6 min

4. The Touching Story 6–8 min

5. Bringing History To Life 7–9 min

Interpretive Reading

1. Read A Story 7–9 min
2. Interpreting Poetry 6–8 min
3. The Monodrama 4–6 min
4. The Play 6–8 min
5. The Oratorical Speech 7–9 min

Interpersonal Communication

1. Conversing With Ease 10–14 min
2. The Successful Negotiator 10–14 min
3. Diffusing Verbal Criticism 10–14 min
4. The Coach 10–14 min
5. Asserting Yourself Effectively 10–14 min

Special Occasion Speeches

1. Mastering The Toast 2–3 min
2. Speaking In Praise 5–7 min
3. The Roast 3–5 min
4. Presenting An Award 3–4 min
5. Accepting An Award 5–7 min

Humorously Speaking

1. Warm Up Your Audience 5–7 min
2. Leave Them With A Smile 5–7 min

3. Make Them Laugh 5–7 min

4. Keep Them Laughing 5–7 min

5. The Humorous Speech 5–7 min

[Courtesy Toastmasters International]

You can see at a glance that public speaking entails a great deal more than merely standing in front of a group.

The advanced manuals present specific areas of interest to the speaker, and help in teaching, as well as reinforcing certain skills desirable in each area. Note also the time limits assigned to the advanced speeches. They are given more leeway to account for the increased information that may need to be presented. This can be a blessing or a curse. For those who feel that five to seven minutes is ridiculously short, they now have an opportunity to speak much longer, depending on the project; conversely, those who feel intimidated by any length of time before an audience, there are so-called advanced speeches that whittle that time down to three minutes (e.g., The Roast or Mastering The Toast).

Whatever your particular objective or interest, there are projects to appeal to just about anyone in any field.

Preparation and Delivery

How do you prepare your speech? Assuming you have selected an appropriate topic that fits the objectives of the speech in question, you now have to create a presentation that will last five to seven minutes. There are several things to consider:

What Shall I Talk About?

I can hear groans from the reader: *I have nothing to say, I don't know anything to talk about, I never graduated college, so I'm not knowledgeable about anything.*

Not true. Consider the following topics:

1. Did I have a good childhood?
2. My love affair with animals.
3. The first time I fell in love.
4. What I did on my ski trip.
5. Why I love camping.
6. Why I do not like sports.
7. What my grandmother was like.
8. Why I love to bake.
9. The biggest regret of my life.
10. Why I loved school.
11. Paint your front door blue.
12. The trouble with camping.

And on and on, ad infinitum. There is never a shortage of topics to talk about. Carry a small notebook with you, and jot down topics as they pop into your head.

Your Target Audience

In a Toastmasters club, your audience are your club members. When you are following the manual projects, it is rarely necessary to consider your audience, per se.

But, if you aspire to give speeches to audiences that are not Toastmasters, or advance to the professional stage, you must consider your target audience. For example, if you are a physician who specializes in pharmaceutical research, hopefully your audience will be like-minded doctors and researchers, or possibly businessmen within the pharmaceutical industry. It would be pointless to give a speech about legalizing marijuana to a group of engineers working on the infrastructure of a city.

Your audience is anyone who is about to listen to your speech. You must structure your speech to fit their interests and expectations in order to be effective.

The Most Powerful Speeches

Some of the best speeches are those that grab the audience and do not let go. That is an umbrella statement that means nothing unless you have experienced its power. What kinds of speeches have those characteristics? They are those that encompass and relate to all humanity, its strengths and weaknesses, its successes and failures. Speeches that have universal appeal are by far the most successful.

So what has universal appeal? Stories.

From time immemorial, society has learned right from wrong through stories. Before the advent of the written word, stories were the fiber that connected people to each other, threading families through generations, unified diverse thoughts into cohesive social networks. Stories are universal. We love them because they touch us. They touch us because they are universal. We recognize ourselves in someone else's foibles, and we empathize. We harken back to a moment in our childhood when we hear the tale of another. We are allowed to identify with one another in a way that is reassuring and comforting. We no longer feel alone in our feelings and emotions.

The best speeches unify. The best speeches tug at our heartstrings in sympathy and move us to action. The best speeches teach us something.

Stories do not have to be fairy tales or fiction. You can include anecdotes to illustrate a point, or make your entire speech a story about something you know. When I wrote the entry on Perseverance in *The Book of Values*, I told the story of the computer class I failed in college. When I began my blog on options trading (http://selling-puts.blogspot.com), I included a page with my own story of having suffered deep losses during the dotcom fiasco (http://selling-puts.blogspot.com/p/the-humbled-trader.html).

Allow yourself to be vulnerable. We all are. Allow yourself to appear true and genuine when you present a talk. Your audience knows what is sincere from what is not. Do not try to snow your audience with false pride. The natural speaker is the one who realizes that they already know, and does not attempt to put on airs. Sincerity is one of the most engaging qualities a public speaker has.

Writing the Speech

The best speeches sound natural and spontaneous. That is because they are. The speaker knows his subject inside out, and speaks with authority. For example, if you have worked as a realtor for the past twenty years, some aspects of the industry are very familiar to you. You should select one segment of the industry, say, financing, and expound on it. If staging a home is your forte, talk about that: what is staging, how to best stage a home to sell, how important staging is in attracting a buyer, etc. Whatever your expertise, talk about that.

Chances are you will want to write your speech. According to the experts, a speech should have a strong opening, a body and a close. I have heard those admonitions so often that they have stopped being meaningful to me. But let us drill down a bit.

A strong opening is your introduction to the speech. For example, "Who Wants To Be a Millionaire?" You want to grab the audience's attention with a few well-placed powerful words. You want your audience's attention to be riveted, and your audience to sit on the edge of their seats ready for the answer to that question.

The body of the speech supports the opening gambit. It is within the body that you expound on your topic of how to become a millionaire.

The close is where you bring all your thoughts together in a short summary, preferably one that will encapsulate in a few words how to put your thoughts into practice. For example, "Abolish debt as the shortest path to a million dollars."

A grave error made by many speakers is trying to memorize their speech word for word. It is a mistake because it does not sound natural or spontaneous. It also opens the door to forgetting, then becoming paralyzed as one scratches one's memory banks to find one's place again.

A far better alternative is to write your speech in general terms, study and trim your speech to the essential elements, then write those elements on index cards and use them as prompts. What you write on the cards should be single words or thoughts – not entire sentences. For example, in the topic on who wants to be a millionaire, you might include such words as DEBT, BUDGET, SAVINGS. As you glance at your cards, each of those words should trigger you to speak about that segment of your speech. This technique makes your talk sound much more spontaneous and candid. Of course, as stated before, you should prepare a speech about something you are familiar with.

Examples and Illustrations

A very effective technique is to sprinkle the body of your speech with examples, just as I have done herein. If you speak about real estate, give examples of different kinds of mortgages; if you speak about horseback riding, give examples of where one can find a dude ranch or learn how to ride. You may also speak about the differences in riding style.

Examples can be given during a speech, just as I have done herein, as well as in the form of handouts and visual aids. For example, I recently gave a talk about the Mediterranean Diet and its role in promoting good health. I prepared a set of slides that flashed on a screen, but I also transferred much of that information to a handout that I printed out and handed to each member of the audience. See the discussion on slides below.

Visual Aids

Some people are very comfortable speaking alongside visual aids, as I am. They prepare slides with pictures or words to support their talk, and control their flow with a remote clicker. The best slides by far are ones that contain only an image and perhaps one or two words, such as the one below:

Your slides are meant to support your talk – not replace it. Assuming you know your topic, you will know what to say in response to such a slide and others in the deck – and so will your audience. The audience will be focusing their attention on you, the speaker, with a mere glance at the slides. Moreover, when the slides are mere suggestions of the topic at any given moment, you are not flashing them quickly one after the other, making it difficult for the audience to follow as their eyes are busy scanning the screen rather than looking and listening to you.

Remember that your audience is listening and watching YOU - not the slides. You do not want to distract your audience; you want to enhance their experience. Your slides should therefore be an adjunct to your talk. Do not fill your slide with too many words that the audience then strains to read just before you toggle to the next slide, leaving them frustrated. For best results, the explanatory words and pictures should appear on the handouts, along with space for notes. This way, the audience can pay attention to your talk, jot down a few words, then study the material at their leisure.

Delivery

I would venture a guess that delivery of a speech is the most intimidating. That is no doubt because of all the things one has to remember, including the content of the speech, the sequence of ideas, as well as a host of other techniques. This can be not only frustrating, but downright off-putting. Consider the many faces of delivering a speech:

1. Write the speech. Select a topic that fits the given project you are working on.
2. Keep your eye on the timing lights and stay within time.
3. Begin your speech with a strong opening, good body and powerful close. An example of an opening is "Why I am a Republican." Then proceed to explain your position, and close with a summary of your speech.
4. Avoid saying uh's, ah's or um's.
5. Make eye contact with the audience.
6. Do not fidget as you present your speech.
7. Use proper gestures.

8. Watch your voice – One of the projects in the Competent Communicator manual is on vocal variety. But this suggestion is about modulating your voice to sound attractive and pleasing to your listeners. Do not drone on monotonously; do not screech in the style of a Hollywood groupie; speak at a rate and volume that are pleasing to the audience. You should practice with family or friends who will give you good feedback.
9. Make sure you speak to the entire audience, not just one person.
10. Watch your posture – Your posture represents your confidence, and the confidence you have in your material. If you slouch or fold your arms over your chest or put your hands in your pockets, you are sending a message to the audience that you lack confidence.
11. Emphasize important points – use slides to reinforce your message or pepper your talk with examples and anecdotes.
12. Don't forget to breathe!

As you can easily see, there are so many moving parts to the delivery of a five-minute speech that many give up before ever starting.

The last item is my own. In my very first club, each time anyone said ah or um, a big nail was dropped into a metal bucket. At another club, a bell was rung as a signal that the speaker had stumbled. The concept was that with such ersatz Pavlovian cues, speakers would become aware of their own stumbling blocks. The problem with such techniques is that they reinforce that behavior, rather than abolish it! They emphasize and underline the unwanted behavior – the very opposite of what they want to accomplish! Needless to say, such tricks are distractions, and the hapless speaker often loses his or her train of thought entirely! Worse, the speaker is intimidated even more, focusing and measuring his or her words, being deliberate and holding their breath – precisely the wrong approach!

Instead of trying to remember all of the above, FORGET EVERYTHING – except what you want to say. None of the above matters as you are learning the tricks of the trade. The only thing that matters is *your speech*. Period. If you say um and ah, so what?! Trust me, no one is going to string you up by your thumbs!

The best advice one can give you as a budding speaker is to be yourself. Do not imitate Colin Powell or another luminary, even if you truly admire him or her. Be yourself. Present yourself, your own speech, your own interests, speak of your own passions. Do not adopt a topic that is currently popular if you do not believe in it or follow it. If you are not interested in football, do not give a speech about it just because the Super Bowl has been in the news lately and you know everyone in your club is interested in football. That is a sure way to struggle with your speech and your delivery.

Time Considerations

One of the items above exhorts you to stay within your time limit. At Toastmasters, meetings typically have a timer who gives various signals to the speaker when he or she is about to reach the time limit. Other organizations have similar activities. The reason that is important is that during competitions, going overtime or not speaking long enough disqualifies a speaker. But outside of speaking organizations, have you noticed congressional hearings with either the Chairman of the

Federal Reserve or anyone else testifying before Congress? They all have timing lights. Each speaker – and indeed, each member of Congress – is given a specific amount of time to ask questions and interact with the person testifying, and he or she, too, is constrained by time. When the Secretary of State testifies to Congress, she was limited to a certain time period within which to answer questions.

Even professional speakers – or perhaps especially professional speakers – are given a time limit to present their talks. If you are invited to speak before a medical group, for example, you will be told that you have 40 or 50 minutes within which to present your talk. Likewise if you are eulogizing someone or giving a toast at a wedding.

Were it not for time limits, people might simply ramble on and on, never getting to the point, perhaps boring their audiences, and certainly not being invited back.

Presenting Your Self

It is my opinion that when you come up to bat, you should present the part. By that I mean that if you are about to speak on the finer points of farming, by all means, dress as a farmer. But for the most part, Toastmasters and other public speaking organizations aim to teach speakers to be professional – not professional speakers, necessarily, but professional in their demeanor. Public speaking is an adjunct to advancing in one's career, and from that standpoint is a professional endeavor. Therefore, it is critical that you learn to present yourself as a professional.

Whether we like it or not, we are judged by our appearance. It may not be fair, but it is a fact:

appearance matters. Look disheveled and you will make a poor impression; dress the part, and likewise you will make an impression.

What kind of impression do you wish to make?

Please do not take this lightly. Yes, we live in an increasingly casual society, but there is a time and place where casual attire is acceptable, and giving a speech is not one of them. Whether you are speaking at your local club or on a professional stage, public speaking is a professional enterprise, and you must look the part.

The Natural Speaker

Natural speakers are a pleasure to behold. They are able to deliver their talk as if it were a conversation with the audience. They are poised, and do not fidget; their gestures are natural instead of forced; they occupy space appropriately, neither standing like a statue nor dancing all over the speaking area; they maintain good eye contact with members of the audience without staring and without flitting from person to person; they maintain the proper distance between themselves and members of the audience, respecting personal spaces; they have great voice control, neither bellowing nor constricting their vocal cords; they are healthy and clean, and dress the part.

If some of the above baffles you, consider how important your physical health is. If you are scheduled to present a day-long seminar beginning at 9:00 a.m., and you spend the previous night drinking and dancing until dawn, the chances are you will feel a bit less than ideal. It is critical, therefore, that you be cognizant of your body and stay away from anything that you know upsets your equilibrium. If you are sensitive to dairy, by all means, avoid it for a couple of days before your talk.

Likewise if you are prone to headaches, avoid all those things which can give you headaches, such as perfumes or alcohol.

The day of your talk, prepare in the best way you know how. Arise calmly, dress and have a light breakfast, brush your teeth, and step in front of your audience prepared. You have your speech on a topic you are an expert on; you slept well; and you have prepared as best you could. The rest is conversation.

Remember that your audience wants you to succeed. Have you ever been a member of an audience where the speaker or performer did *not* do well? How did that make you feel? I venture to say you felt embarrassed. This is part of the empathy we feel as human beings. That is why we always want our presenters to do well. We subconsciously root for them, because we vicariously live through them. We see ourselves in their place.

The Pregnant Pause

Silence is powerful. And silence is an art. It is the art of knowing when to pause for emphasis, when to pause for effect, when to pause to give the audience a chance to digest your last statement, when to pause to let them laugh at your last joke. It is almost as difficult to master the art of silence as it is to master the art of comedy, but it can be learned and applied skillfully, as long as you endeavor to always be kind and empathetic with your audience.

The Qualifier

Many speakers believe that they are attractive to the audience when they self-deprecate and excuse their lack of experience. Such opening statements as "I'm sorry, I've never done this before" detract from you, the presenter. Even if it is true that you have never given a speech, or never sung in public, or stepping onto the stage for the very first time, there is no need to inform the audience ahead of time.

That is a fundamental truth of being a natural speaker. Remember the discussion about sincerity and vulnerability: The audience is rooting for you. The audience is a group of human beings who have similar problems and frailties as you and me. The audience wants you to succeed, and putting yourself down as a way of garnering their sympathy makes you appear less than forthright.

The Power – and Danger – in Comedy

People love to laugh. Laughing feels good, increases endorphins and plays a role in uniting a disparate audience. Speakers frequently resort to telling jokes as part of their talk, sometimes opening their presentation with a joke, or more likely peppering their talk with some levity.

As all successful comics will tell you, comedy is an art that when delivered well will enchant, but will fall like a bomb if badly delivered. Comedy depends on timing, the turn of a phrase, and on the topic itself. A solemn affair rarely lends itself to guffaws. Comedy can be cutting and mean or self-deprecating and light hearted. If you are the presenter, err on the side of self-deprecation or no joking at all, to be safe. Unless you know your audience, be circumspect with the use of levity. There are many situations which are obviously offensive, and many more which can be interpreted as offensive. You do not want to encounter either one.

Be extra judicious in your use of irony and mirth, lest you offend someone's sensibilities. You do not want an evaluation to come back with "That wasn't funny!"

Evaluations

Toastmasters International has in place a system of feedback where each formal speech is evaluated by a member of the group. Evaluation is an art: The object of an evaluation is to point out what the speaker did well, as well as where the speaker could improve. But the evaluators themselves are Toastmasters, with their own set of skills and their own deficiencies. An evaluation is merely one person's opinion – it is not written in stone, and the speaker should not necessarily hang his or her entire speaking career upon one evaluation.

In my experience, the tendency at Toastmasters is to whitewash flaws in the spirit of not hurting the speaker's feelings. While I do not advocate being abrupt or hurtful in any way, I do prefer honest feedback.

The evaluator has only two to three minutes to deliver his evaluation. That is not much time. There are various techniques for an effective evaluation: the "sandwich" method, in which the evaluator says something positive about the speaker, then introduces an area for improvement, and concludes with an encouraging remark. Another technique is to speak about what the evaluator heard, saw and felt: How did the speech impress the evaluator; how did the speaker appear as he or she delivered the speech; and how that speech/speaker made the evaluator feel.

Techniques abound in delivering effective evaluations. The crux of an evaluation is critical listening, remaining attentive during the speech, taking notes, and paying attention to the objectives in the manual for the given speech. For example, if the objectives are getting familiar with visual aids, yet the speaker presents a haphazard speech on how he or she spent his summer vacation without the benefit of props or visual aids, clearly the objectives of the speech were not met, and the speaker should be so apprised. This is a case where the speaker should not receive credit for that speech, and should be requested to repeat it – although my experience has been that that rarely happens.

Evaluations are a source of feedback to the speaker. They are meant to help the speaker improve. They are meant to encourage and sustain, rally the speaker to perform better next time, and spur the speaker onward. If the speaker was superb, do not shy away from telling him or her exactly what you think. If you are hard pressed to find an area for improvement, do not invent one.

The Role of the Evaluator

As valuable as evaluations are for the speaker, especially when given sincerely and straightforwardly, evaluations also serve the evaluator. How? Consider that an evaluation is a mini-speech! And it is also an impromptu speech! The evaluator must listen critically, read and assimilate the parameters of the speech project being delivered, and must address various aspects of the speech: Has the speaker met his or her objectives as stated in the manual? Is the speech content well written, with a strong opening, body and close? Is the topic appropriate?

There is some debate as to whether the evaluator should evaluate the speaker or the speech itself. The two cannot be separated. The speech itself must fit certain criteria, but so does the speaker. Eye contact has been stressed within these pages; addressing the entire audience – not just focusing on one or two members of the audience; projecting proper voice control, volume and pitch; using appropriate gestures – all these characteristics belong to the speaker.

The role of the evaluator is one that combines everything he or she sees or hears, and then, given the evaluator's own skill, must give feedback in a diplomatic and sensitive manner, neither whitewashing trouble spots nor hitting the hapless speaker with a sledgehammer.

An example of an evaluation might sound something like this:

"I very much enjoyed your take on the plight of the wolf in Yosemite Park. You gave us a great picture of the life cycle of the wolf and its place in the ecosystem, information that I was not aware of. Your voice sounded firm and strong, and you included the entire audience in your story. I observed that everyone was watching you intently as you spoke, so obviously you had the audience's rapt attention.

"May I suggest that you include the audience sitting in the wings as well. You had a tendency to speak to the center of the room.

"You stayed within your time limit, which is admirable; but a story such as yours requires a great deal more detail that I would love to hear about. Perhaps you would agree to give a continuation of that speech for another project. Thank you for your speech. Great job."

The above example of an evaluation assumes that in fact the speaker did a great job, and that those words truly represent your assessment. There is nothing worse than receive insincere feedback – the speaker feels it, and the audience senses that which is not genuine and true. Tell the truth, and study the art of tact and diplomacy in rendering an evaluation for a speech that is less than wonderful. You, as the evaluator, will grow greatly with the knowledge of how to deliver a "corrective" critique without offending the receiving party.

Thank You

There is some debate as to whether or not the speaker should say "thank you" to the audience at the end of his or her speech. Some experts in the field of public speaking claim that it is the audience who should thank the speaker, but I bend more in the direction that you can never go wrong saying thank you, in any circumstance. Thank you for coming; thank you for listening to me; thank you for being there so I may deliver my speech – any or all of it is appropriate.

And I thank you for reading this book.

◆ ◆ ◆

Please feel free to contact me, to give me your impressions of the content, to write a review on Amazon, or for anything else. My website is http://Pro-Wordsmith.net, and my email address is Prowriter33@gmail.com

About The Author

I am a child of the world: My grandparents were Turkish, my mother French, my father Tunisian, and my husband is Japanese. I was born in Israel. Suffice to say that such a multicultural foundation has created a deep understanding of the subtleties and nuances of language and culture.

My international background, and all the cultures that have melded into my upbringing, have shaped my love of reading and writing. I write about subjects that I love, ranging from music to nutrition and trading options on the stock market.

It may be confounding to try to figure out what is my expertise, until one realizes that we are all endowed with varied tastes and moods which change over time. I am equally at home writing fantasy stories as I am explaining the nuances of stock options to anyone who would listen.

My schooling began in Israel, and continued in Paris, then in the United States. I graduated Florida International University with studies in psychology, statistics, international finance, languages, eventually earning my degree in psychology with honors. It was during my graduate classes in psychology that I fell in love with the exacting process of research, writing and editing academic papers.

I have written extensively as a ghostwriter, as well as under my own byline, and have published 22 books, five under a pseudonym. A new nom-de-plume is M. Carling, my alter ego for this and subsequent works of fiction.

My latest book, "It Ain't The Money! The Success Mindset of Great Leaders" in in print, eBook and Audio formats. For more information, please peruse my website at http://Pro-Wordsmith.net, or contact me at Prowriter33@gmail.com.

I am rather shy, so to overcome my reservations, I learned to speak in public. My story can be found in the Introduction to this book. I have since taken charge of the erratic butterflies, and corral them to fly in formation when I stand before a group!